Welcome to the Backyard

by Ruth Owen

Published in 2016 by Ruby Tuesday Books Ltd.

Editor: Mark J. Sachner
Designer: Emma Randall
Consultant: Judy Wearing, PhD, BEd
Production: John Lingham

Photo credits:
Alamy: 9 (top), 15 (right), 19 (bottom), 22, 26; FLPA: 4 (bottom left), 8 (bottom), 11, 17 (right), 23, 30; Shutterstock: Cover, 2–3, 4 (top), 4 (bottom right), 5, 6–7, 8 (top), 9 (bottom), 10, 12–13, 14, 16, 17 (left), 18, 19 (top), 20–21, 24–25, 27, 28–29, 30, 31; Wikipedia Creative Commons: 15 (left).

Library of Congress Control Number: 2015916857

ISBN 978-1-910549-62-9

Printed and published in the United States of America

For further information including rights and permissions requests, please contact our Customer Service Department at 877-337-8577.

Contents

Words shown in **bold** in the text are explained in the glossary.

Welcome to the Backyard

Who and what lives in a backyard?

This **habitat** can be home to trees, grass, and other plants.

The residents of this habitat include **insects**, birds, and other animals.

The plants and animals get what they need to live from the backyard.

A backyard is a type of ecosystem. An ecosystem includes all the living things in an area. It also includes non-living things such as sunlight, rain, and soil. Everything in an ecosystem has its own part to play.

So let's find out what happens in this little neighborhood …
… welcome to the backyard!

Spring Is Here!

It's early spring, and the snow in the backyard is finally melting.

As the weather gets warmer, daffodil plants appear from underground.

Bud

Apple tree branch

Daffodils

Leaves

Blossoms

In spring, buds grow on the bare branches of the trees. When the buds burst open, leaves and blossoms uncurl from inside.

Sunflower seeds

All over the yard, there are **seeds** waiting in the soil.

People plant seeds, too.

When the spring sunshine warms the soil, the seeds grow into new plants.

A flower bud grows.

A sunflower seedling grows from the soil.

The sunflower plant grows bigger.

What do you think happens once new plants start to grow?

Lots of Plants to Eat

The juicy new leaves and **shoots** soon attract hungry animals.

Snails slowly slide from plant to plant, munching on leaves.

Snail

Aphid

Stem

Tiny insects called aphids suck sweet juices from leaves and stems.

All winter, ladybugs have been keeping warm in sheltered places.

Now that spring has arrived, they get busy eating aphids and other insects.

Ladybugs inside dry, dead plant stems

Aphid

A ladybug lives for about one year. During that time, it can eat up to 5,000 aphids!

Ladybug

Why are birds very busy in spring?

It's Time to Build Nests

A female robin is collecting twigs and dry grass in the backyard.

She uses these materials to build a nest in the old apple tree.

Then she lays four blue eggs in the nest.

Robin

Once a robin has laid her eggs, she sits on them to keep them warm. It takes about 14 days for robin chicks to grow inside their eggs.

Robin eggs

In the toolshed, a mouse is looking for a cozy place to build her nest.

What busy insect is buzzing from flower to flower in the backyard?

Busy Bees

Bees visit backyard plants to drink sweet **nectar** from their flowers.

As they do this, the little insects help the plants. How?

Bee

Pollen

Flowers produce a dust called pollen.

Many plants need pollen from a different plant in order to produce seeds.

As a bee searches for nectar in a plant's flower, pollen sticks to its fuzzy body.

Then the bee carries the pollen to other flowers.

The transfer of pollen from one plant's flower to another is called **pollination**. Flowers need bees to pollinate them so they can produce seeds. Bees need flowers for food. It's a perfect partnership!

There's another colorful insect with wings that pollinates flowers. Can you name it?

Butterflies and Caterpillars

It's not only bees that feed on nectar—butterflies do, too.

A butterfly sucks up nectar through its long, straw-like mouthpart.

As it flutters around the yard, a butterfly also carries pollen from flower to flower.

Mouthpart

Lots of different backyard insects pollinate plants, including butterflies, moths, wasps, flies, and beetles.

A painted lady butterfly

A female butterfly lays her eggs on the leaves of plants.

As soon as caterpillars hatch from the eggs, they start munching on the leaves!

Caterpillar

Painted lady butterfly eggs

Why is a rainy day a good thing in the backyard?

A Rainy Day

Drip, drip, splish, splash—it's a rainy day in the backyard.

Every plant and animal in the yard needs water to live.

A wasp sips from the raindrops that collect on a blade of grass.

Roots

The rainwater trickles down into the soil. Now the trees, grass, sunflowers, and other plants can take in the water they need with their roots.

A thirsty robin drinks rainwater that collects in a birdbath.

It washes its dusty feathers, too.

After dark, a fox visits the yard to drink from the birdbath!

What wriggly garden animal helps plants get water?

Welcome to a Worm's World

The backyard's soil is home to hundreds of earthworms.

Worms eat soil and dead plant material such as rotting leaves.

Inside their bodies, worms turn this mixture into poop, called worm castings.

Earthworms

Rotting leaves

Worm castings

Worm castings are filled with lots of **nutrients** that plants need to grow and be healthy.

Plants take in the nutrients through their roots.

As worms wriggle through the soil, their bodies make tunnels and holes. Rainwater trickles down into the soil through these tiny spaces. Once the water is underground, plants can reach it with their roots.

Roots

Tunnel

What backyard residents hunt for worms to eat?

Worms for Dinner!

In the old apple tree, the robin chicks have hatched from their eggs.

Now the mother and father robin must find lots of food for their babies.

The father robin tugs a worm from the soil.

Then he flies to the nest and feeds it to the hungry chicks.

Father robin

Mother robin

Chick

Adult robins eat worms, snails, and insects such as caterpillars. They also feed on berries.

What baby animals do you think are living in the toolshed?

Babies in the Toolshed

In the toolshed, baby mice huddle together in their flowerpot nest.

Baby mice

Mother mouse

The mother mouse filled the flowerpot with dry grass and moss she found in the yard.

She feeds the tiny babies with milk from her body.

The mother mouse eats seeds she finds in the shed.

She searches for food such as seeds, fruit, worms, and snails in the yard, too.

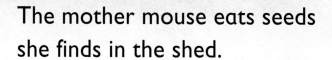
Bean seeds

Foxes hunt for mice, rabbits, squirrels, and birds. Sometimes they eat snails, worms, and insects. They also eat fruit and raid trash cans to find scraps of food.

As she scampers around the yard, she must hide from foxes and pet cats that try to eat her!

What other backyard animals eat seeds?

23

It's Time for Seeds and Fruit

Sunflower seeds

It's summer, and plants are producing seeds.

A goldfinch

All around the backyard, birds are feeding on the seeds.

Some seeds drop from a flower to the soil. Others are blown to a new growing place. Next spring, some of these seeds will grow into new plants.

Dandelion seeds

Lilac seeds

The apple tree's seeds have formed inside juicy fruits.

People pick some of the apples and make apple sauce and pies.

What do you think happens to the apple tree in fall?

Autumn Days

When fall arrives, the apple tree drops its leaves and fruit.

Once the apples rot, the seeds inside may grow into new trees.

Some of the rotting apples become food for mice, birds, and other animals.

26

Dead leaves and flowers lie on the soil and become food for worms and snails.

Tiny woodlice scuttle over the cold ground feeding on the dead plants, too.

Woodlouse

Woodlice live under stones and logs where it's damp. These little creatures belong to an animal group called **crustaceans**. They are related to crabs and shrimp.

When winter comes, how do people help birds find food?

Winter Comes Around

Before the first snow, people plant **bulbs** in the backyard soil.

In spring, daffodils will grow from the bulbs.

Daffodil bulb

During winter, many plants look as if they have died. They are just resting, though. When the weather warms up in spring, they will grow new shoots and leaves.

Once snow covers the yard, it's difficult for birds to find food.

People help birds by hanging feeders from trees.

Birds visit the feeders to get a meal of seeds.

Bird feeder

Northern cardinal

For now, the garden is white and still.

But soon it will be spring again ....

A Backyard Food Web

A food web is a diagram that shows who eats who in an ecosystem.

Some of the animals in a backyard eat plants.

Others feed on their neighbors.

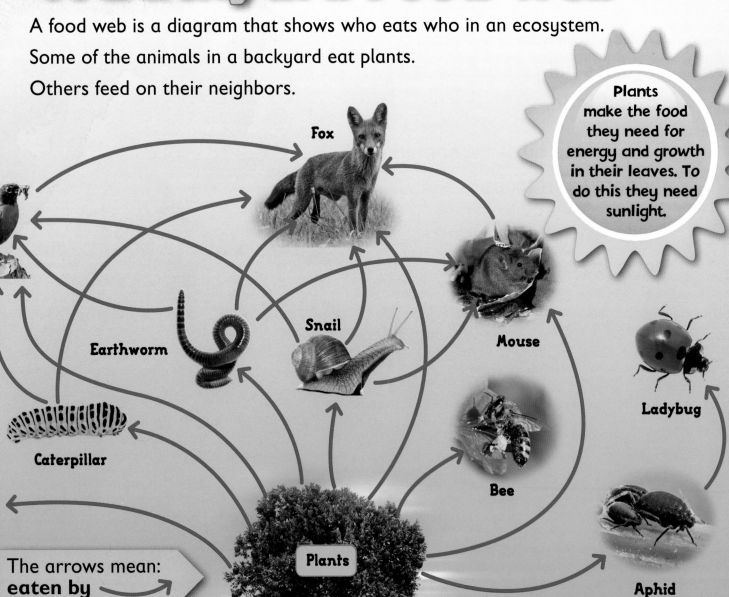

Plants make the food they need for energy and growth in their leaves. To do this they need sunlight.

Fox

Bird

Earthworm

Snail

Mouse

Ladybug

Caterpillar

Bee

Woodlouse

Plants

Aphid

The arrows mean: eaten by

Glossary

bulb (BUHLB) The rounded underground part that some plants grow from. Food for the new plant is stored in the bulb.

crustacean (kruhs-TAY-shun) A member of an animal group that has jointed legs and a thick, hard shell, called an exoskeleton.

habitat (HAB-uh-tat) The place where an animal or plant lives. A habitat can be a backyard, a forest, a desert, or the ocean.

insect (IN-sekt) An animal with six legs, a body in three sections, and a hard shell called an exoskeleton.

nectar (NEK-tur) A sugary liquid that flowers produce to attract insects and other animals. When animals visit flowers to feed on nectar, they help pollinate them.

nutrient (NOO-tree-uhnt) A substance that a living thing needs to grow, get energy, and stay healthy.

pollination (pol-uh-NAY-shuhn) The transfer of pollen between flowers to help plants produce seeds.

seed (SEED) A tiny part of a flower that contains all the material needed to grow a new plant.

shoot (SHOOT) A new part that grows on a plant. Shoots can become new stems or leaves.

Index

Read More

Lawrence, Ellen. *What Lily Gets from Bee: And Other Pollination Facts (Plant-ology)*. New York: Bearport Publishing (2013).

Loewen, Nancy. *Garden Wigglers: Earthworms in Your Backyard*. Mankato, MN: Picture Window Books (2006).

Learn More Online

To learn more about backyard animals and plants, go to
www.rubytuesdaybooks.com/habitats